HOW CAN I CHANGE FOR HEAVEN'S SAKE?

HOW CAN I CHANGE

A PRACTICAL 10-STEP PLAN TO IMPROVE THE ABC'S (ATTITUDE, BEHAVIOR, AND CHARACTER) OF YOUR LIFE

FOR HEAVEN'S SAKE?

RABBI DONIEL FRANK

FELDHEIM PUBLISHERS
JERUSALEM NEW YORK

ISBN 978-1-59826-595-8

Page layout by Eden Chachamtzedek

Distributed by:

FELDHEIM PUBLISHERS
POB 43163 / Jerusalem, Israel

208 Airport Executive Park
Nanuet, NY 10954

www.feldheim.com

10 9 8 7 6 5 4 3 2 1

Printed in Israel

הרב אהרן פעלדמאן
RABBI AHARON FELDMAN
409 YESHIVA LANE, BALTIMORE, MD 21208
TEL.: 410-6539433 FAX: 410-6534694
STUDY: 410-4847200 EXT. 114

ROSH HAYESHIVA
NER ISRAEL RABBINICAL COLLEGE

ראש הישיבה
ישיבת נר ישראל

בס"ד ח באייר תש"ע

APPROBATION

Rabbi Doniel Frank has written a book of great merit and benefit. Utilizing the vehicle of a series of conversations during *Aseres Yemey Teshuva* between a true "seeker of G-d" and a wise mentor, we follow the development of the seeker into a true *Oved Hashem*.

The book has the effect of a road-map for spiritual growth and teaches many lessons which every reader will be able to apply to his own spiritual growth –provided he, too, is interested in growing.

It is my hope that this book will be widely read and applied.

Aharon Feldman

Rabbi Aharon Feldman

Contents

In memory of

מרדכי דוד בן חנוך יחיאל

צירל בת יחיאל מיכל

יהודה בן חיים

דבורה בת אהרון

זכרונם לברכה

From their children,
Irving and Rachel Frank,
grandchildren, and great-grandchildren

In memory of

יהושע בן אהרון צבי

אברהם אייזיק בן יוסף

שינא משא בת חיים שמואל

זכרונם לברכה

From their children,
Chaim and Hali Gottesman,
grandchildren, and great-grandchildren

About this little book that took such a long time to write...

THIS BOOK IS A project that began over twenty years ago. I had written the first draft — a series of essays — when I was still a student in yeshivah. Though I was satisfied with its content, I held onto the manuscript. I was not ready to make it public.

For one thing, as I saw it, it had no personality; just information. I have an aversion to lectures, on whatever side of the lectern, and, essentially, that is what the book was, at that point.

But there was more that was missing, though I could not tell what. It just did not seem complete.

So it sat... and sat.

Two careers later, I stand ready to print.

For as I interacted with people in my role as a rabbi, and then again in my career as a family therapist, the material that I had written as a young yeshivah boy was coming alive, being supported, enriched, and, yes, challenged, by scores of insights and stories that grew out of the many discussions I had had with clients and congregants, as well as with mentors of my own. As I became more practiced in the process of growth, I included the resulting knowledge acquired by those experiences in the text. Consequently, as I evolved, so did the manuscript, as it ultimately morphed from a collection of essays into an emotional dialogue between a searching man and his wise mentor.

Who is the man and who is his mentor? There is no one answer, for they are each composites of the vast number of seekers and mentors I have been privileged to know, all of whom deserve to be credited as contributors to this book.

Still, a few specific acknowledgments are in order.

- First, to my most important mentors, my parents, **Mr. and Mrs. Irving and Rachel Frank**, and my in-laws, **Rabbi and Mrs. Chaim and Hali Gottesman**, who are always a source of loving support and guidance in all that I do
- To **HaRav Yaakov Weinberg**, *zt"l,* my Rosh HaYeshivah, who, aside from serving a lead role in my life as my spiritual mentor, expressed support of this project during its early stages, and whose insight on growing "for Heaven's Sake" serves as the foundational concept of this book
- To **Rabbi Aharon Feldman, Rabbi Tzvi Berkowitz, Rabbi Dr. Abraham J. Twerski** and **Dr. David Pelcovitz**, who reviewed the manuscript and made

suggestions that helped ensure that the contents were sound from both a Torah and psychological perspective; to **Rabbi Chaim Schabes** for his help with the sources; and to my good friend **Rabbi Label Lam** for articulating the distinction between hypocrite and "work in progress," as well as providing the analogy of the vandalizing teen on the subway

- To my brother, **Howie Frank**, whose many suggestions helped shape the final product, not the least of which was to keep the process of growth real, relevant, and personal
- To my brother-in-law, **Rabbi Boruch Leff**, for reviewing the manuscript and sharing his publishing expertise with me
- To **Rabbi Yisroel Y. Krohn** for permission to use the translation of the *Al Chet Viduy* from his booklet, *Viduy* (Feldheim Publishers)
- To **Charlotte Friedland** (editing), **Ben Gasner** (cover design), **Eden Chachamtzedek** (typesetting), **Rabbi Dovid Rossoff** (publishing), and **Eli Meir Hollander** at **Feldheim** (distributing) for adding their talent and insight to this book.

Why publish now? To be sure, I was tempted to hang onto the manuscript even longer, as I go on with my work and continue to learn. But it was time.

I knew this because my wife, **Shevi,** insisted six months

ago that it was time and urged me to print. In that way, she provided the vision and force behind making this book a reality. This, as with any of my other accomplishments, is a product of her support and encouragement, wisdom and humility... and for all of that I dedicate this book to her.

May we have the strength and wisdom to guide our children—**Tziri**, **Shua**, **Miri**, **Tamar**, **Yehudis**, **Mordechai Dovid**, and **Shaina**—towards a life of ongoing personal growth, *for Heaven's Sake*!

Donny Frank
Spring Valley, New York
Sivan 5770/May 2010

The Challenge of Change

WE ALL WANT TO grow; we all want to improve; we all want to be the best that we can be. It is a drive that is intrinsic to the soul that we possess. But in order to grow we have to change the way we do things, and that is not easy. It takes time — *but who has the time*? It takes work — *but who has the energy*? And even when we have the time and energy, it requires a plan — *but where can we find one*?

So we drop the ball and move on with life — until something motivates us to change. Sometimes change happens through inspiration; sometimes it is triggered by guilt or pressure from others; and sometimes, it happens when we hit rock bottom and get fed up with the way things have been...

The Awakening

IT HAD BEEN A long, hard, and backbreaking day, with four prayers down and one to go. The rabbi, draped in his *talis,* solemnly stepped up to the pulpit to deliver the year's most meaningful message. The drama of the moment was written all over his face and on those of his anxious congregants, who were sitting up and ready to hear their charge. And as the rabbi uttered his first words, it all started to sink in.

"The gates are closing. This is the time to make your commitments!" beckoned the rabbi. "Make the final confession during these closing moments of Yom Kippur your most sincere..."

One man heard the words "commitments" and "most sincere" and began to feel faint. Yes, on the one hand, he nodded in agreement and got ready to "roll up his sleeves" to face the task at hand.

But at the same time, he sensed that "commitments" and "sincere confessions" are the products of focused energy and lots of hard work. And when he realized that he had not done any of that, his drive and inspiration turned into panic and despair. He stood pitifully unprepared, and wondered how it was possible to ready himself on such short notice for the enormity of the *Ne'ilah* experience.

In short, he simply did not feel that he belonged to that holy and awesome moment.

But just then, this desperate moment produced a glimmer of hope: he was actually experiencing his first pangs of real regret! The imagery generated by the weakening sun and the liturgical references to the closing gates were beginning to penetrate the hardened shell of his heart. He kicked himself as he wondered why he let all those days go by without working towards this fateful moment. He berated himself for not having taken advantage of the past forty days since the beginning of Elul— a time when G-d actively desires man's repentance. He yearned for the opportunity to do them all over again as he stood so painfully embarrassed before his Creator.

He thought to himself how different the experience might have been had he prepared. "Maybe if I had a paper in hand—something concrete detailing the work I had done to improve myself and the commitments I had thought through—I could declare, with some degree of honesty, that things would be different this year. I could have been standing here with more confidence." He allowed these thoughts to fill his mind and the regret became unbearable.

He took a deep breath and tried to return his attention to the rabbi when yet another sobering thought took hold of him: "I really have no idea *how* to change; I would not know *what* to do even if I could take the time to do it!"

Now certainly, over the years, he had been inundated with inspirational talks about the importance of *teshuvah* and had learned about the steps that it must include. But he was never shown a practical plan, a roadmap of sorts that would help him navigate the process of personal growth and integrate its concepts into his life in a real and meaningful way. He would have to find a mentor — perhaps a great rabbi, or just someone wise — who would take the time to walk him through it. And that would be his commitment, yes, that would be it! He had worked things through after all!

So, the rabbi had succeeded. Not quite the way that he intended, but nonetheless, he got that man to cry, with real tears, for being so unprepared, and ready to commit to finding a mentor who would teach him a way to change. These thoughts and feelings formed the mission that would propel him through that *Ne'ilah,* and give him the sense that he actually *did* belong to that holy moment.

His only hope was that if he prayed hard enough, G-d would grant him an extension for *teshuvah* and atonement on credit. After all, only G-d would know the depth of his regret and how he would spare no effort to search for that mentor, wherever he may be, as soon as he would break his fast...

LIFE BECAME BUSY after Yom Kippur, and as the days had turned into weeks, and the weeks into months, the man remained the same as he had always been, in spite of all of the heart-wrenching commitments he had made on that fateful day. Now and then, he reflected on how fleeting those moments of inspiration had been. Considering the intensity of the experience he had gone through, who would have imagined that he still would be procrastinating this way?

Of course, he had spoken with many people about his resolve to find a mentor for personal growth. But in the absence of the emotions of *Ne'ilah,* it remained mere table talk. Even when a friend gave him a promising lead about a local "wise man" who was reputed to have a plan, he did nothing more than to write down the phone number and tuck it away.

IT WAS NOT until the opening night of *Selichos* the following year, when he was moved by a talk about the importance of *teshuvah,* that he was prompted to act. The fear of repeating last year's *Ne'ilah* experience was palpable enough to motivate him to begin his search for real.

But where would he begin? A whole year had gone by and there were only days left until Rosh Hashanah. Just then he remembered about his potential mentor, whose contact information he had scribbled on a scrap of paper. Now if only he could remember who tipped him off or where he put the number. He quickly fumbled through his wallet and, by minor miracle, was able to find it. He wasted no time getting to a phone to set up an appointment. His heart raced as he reached for the receiver and began to dial. His finger flew fervently across the keypad, but when the line began to ring, he suddenly hesitated.

"Surely the wise man is busy with his own preparations for his own personal growth," he thought. "I ought to hang up and wait until after Yom Kippur. It's not right to impose myself on him on such short notice. For now, I'll make a *real* commitment to call him *right* away, even before I break my fast."

He had himself convinced—but it was too late. The wise man had already answered the phone, and by the call's end, they were scheduled to meet the very next day.

The series of meetings over the next ten days changed the man's life profoundly in many ways. There is so much that the wise man had taught him during that time, not the least of which was to share a good thing with others. So, in that spirit, he decided to make public his firsthand, candid account of that ten-day encounter with his mentor. It reflects the Ten-Step Plan as he experienced it that first year. His hope is that others will also benefit from his mentor's system for change as he did—for Heaven's sake.

The Roadmap

I WAS APPREHENSIVE AS I rang the doorbell. But those feelings were short-lived, as the wise man's warm greetings and kind compliments made me feel much more at ease. He told me that he was impressed with my commitment to personal growth. He never questioned why I came, or why I chose him as my mentor.

We walked into the dining room and sat at the table. He began to speak almost immediately, as though he had something to confess. "I must tell you from the start," he began, "that this plan is comprised of concepts and strategies that are not my own. They are all taken from our holy writings. All I did was to organize the information in a manner that is most meaningful to me."

This was no surprise to me. I had never doubted that all there was to know was to be found in our sacred literature. What I needed was a kind of roadmap to navigate my course.

"There is little time until Rosh Hashanah and I know I should have called you much earlier," I began. "I would fully understand if you kept things simple for now. We can always stay in touch throughout the year if I need to fill in any of the gaps."

"I appreciate your consideration, but the plan is a simple one—that is, to teach. Implementing it is the hard work and that you will do on your own. I had no intention of spending more than a few minutes with you each day." He paused. "Of course, if you have any other matters you would like to speak about, we might find time for them as well."

I was surprised—and a bit disappointed. How could anything truly brilliant be given over in such short time? Besides, even if it could, how would I be able to implement his teachings on my own? I was beginning to wonder whether I had really found my man...

Meanwhile, my mentor reached for the first volume of Maimonides' *Mishneh Torah* and began flipping through its pages.

"Let me show you the roadmap, as you have called it, for the next ten days. It's just one line in the section on the laws of *teshuvah*..." he spoke as he leafed through its pages, looking for the place. "Ah, here it is." He turned to me and began to read:

> Please G-d; I have sinned; I have transgressed; I have committed iniquity before You by doing such-and-such. And

> behold, I regret and am ashamed for what I have done. And I am committed never to repeat this act. (1:1)

As I copied these words into my notepad, my mind began to race. I had seen this statement many times before, but never viewed it as a prescription for *Aseres Y'mei Teshuvah.* I was excited to hear more.

My mentor continued: "Each phrase in this carefully formulated statement represents a different stop on the road towards change. And the goal for these ten days is to arrive at Yom Kippur having addressed them all, one at a time.

MY MIND, NOW in overdrive, was already sorting out the elements of the Rambam's confession. I thought out loud:

"There is admitting to the wrongdoing, specifying the wrongdoing, expressing remorse, and resolving for the future. Did I get that right?"

"Mostly," my mentor responded.

"'Mostly?' What did I leave out?"

Convinced that I had gotten them all, I reread the passage several times. But as far as I could tell, there were only four parts to the confession.

"Let me help," he offered. "You began with 'admitting to the wrongdoing.' Now, tell me, with which word does that begin?"

"'*Chatasi* — I sinned.'"

"Correct, but that is the *third* Hebrew word of the confession! Why did the Rambam start with the first two words?"

"'*Ana Hashem* — Please G-d?'" I thought for a moment. "To me, it seems like just some sort of salutation."

"Perhaps. But the Rambam wastes no words: the salutation, as you call it, must surely be a critical component of the confession."

I nodded in agreement.

"Time is tight so I will tell you my thoughts on this matter. The words '*Ana Hashem*' are certainly critical to the confession. That is because when the Torah speaks about confession, it says that we must confess '*before G-d,*' and it is with these words that we fulfill that requirement."

"But isn't that obvious?" I interrupted. "I mean, after all, to whom else would we direct our confession?"

"To ourselves, of course," my mentor replied nonchalantly.

There was a pause. He could tell that I was confused.

"DURING OUR PHONE conversation yesterday," he continued gently, "do you remember how you kept apologizing for inconveniencing me during this time of year?"

"Yes."

"And do you remember that you said you could wait until after Rosh Hashanah—because, as you put it, that's the time *teshuvah* begins?"

"I do," I said, now fully aware that I was being led down the road of self-incrimination.

"Well, with all due respect, that is where you made your mistake. You see, since Rosh Hashanah makes up two of the Ten Days of *Teshuvah,* a significant part of this period, it must, somehow, mandate some kind of *teshuvah* work.

"Still, your mistake was an understandable one. Even the Rosh Hashanah *machzor* makes no overt references to *teshuvah* at all. No confessions or regrets, no chest-beating. Compare that to Yom Kippur, the last of the ten days, when we have no less than ten confessions and a running theme of *teshuvah* throughout its prayers. We are left to wonder: what exactly *is* the game plan for Rosh Hashanah?"

I sat still, waiting for the answer.

My mentor seemed to contemplate the question, and then unfolded his thoughts. "There are Rosh Hashanah commitments and there are New Year's resolutions: if you look carefully, you will find that there is an enormous difference between the two."

"Just a semantic difference to me," I said, with a touch of defiance.

"Not at all," he insisted. "The highest-ranking New Year's

resolutions typically include things like quitting smoking, losing weight, getting organized, and buying a membership in the local health club. Yet, without formal polls, a hunch tells me that this list hardly represents the most common commitments made by Jews around Rosh Hashanah time. Instead, as Jews, we tend to commit to things like not speaking *lashon hara,* praying with a *minyan,* and increasing our Torah learning. Would you agree?"

I nodded.

"Now, why is there this difference? Surely, it is important for Jews to take care of their health. Smoking is dangerous. Being overweight is a leading cause of heart disease. Exercising, among other things, awakens the mind and makes one more alert to perform *mitzvos* to the fullest. If so, why are these lists so drastically different?"

"I'm not really sure," I admitted.

"The difference, as I see it, is plain and simple. There are resolutions that are made to make you feel better about yourself, and there are those intended to bring you closer to G-d. When someone thinks, 'I want to be healthy; I want to look good; I want to feel good' or 'I'm disappointed in myself and want to feel accomplished,' he commits to doing things that will make him feel good about himself. And when he makes those commitments, he is his own audience.

"On the other hand, one who views all of his behaviors in the context of his relationship with G-d asks, 'How can

I get closer to my Creator?' When his misdeeds are seen in this light and his motivation to correct them is to reconnect to G-d—that is the thinking that underlies *teshuvah.* He is changing his life for Heaven's sake."

"I understand the point you're making," I began, "but why can't New Year's resolutions—the very ones you gave as examples—be used for Rosh Hashanah as well? You yourself said that taking care of our health is something G-d would want. Why don't we use that as a means to reconnect with Him?"

"Excellent point," my mentor conceded. "And the truth is that they can. Those issues *can* be on our list too. For instance, a Jew who smokes seriously ought to consider stopping. But because this kind of behavior is not as overtly spiritual as those that are explicit *mitzvos,* it takes greater effort to frame it with an '*Ana Hashem.*' Naturally, if that effort is made as a commitment to come closer to G-d, it can be just as effective as any other *mitzvah.* Connecting with G-d is our highest calling. All meaningful change must begin in that framework."

AS I FELT I was finally getting the concept of a "frame," I picked up the point: "Are you suggesting that Rosh Hashanah functions as the '*Ana Hashem*' for the *teshuvah* process?"

"Exactly!" cried my mentor. "It's the critical first step of *teshuvah.* By crystallizing our motivation, we feel true regret and create the frame to commit to new behaviors. And the way to do that is by spending Rosh Hashanah reflecting on our relationship with G-d. That is the day's calling. We have to allow its *mitzvos* and prayers to penetrate our hearts and minds, and permit the enormity of these days to make us aware of the full reality of our privileged relationship with G-d. We remind ourselves that He is our Creator, King, Judge, Father, Master, and that each of these titles means that He relates to us in a unique and special way..."

He paused. Then he sat back and assumed a pondering position, as he contemplated the direction in which he wished to take this discussion. Clearly he had more to say. But, a few reflective moments later, it seemed that he had decided that, for now, he had said enough. He had explained the imperative of the first days of the coming ten days that would lead me to *teshuvah*. So he stood up and escorted me out the door.

We reached my car, and he offered these final words of advice: "Remember, reflection is the key to these next two days of Rosh Hashanah. Keep your mind present throughout the prayers: Empty yourself out beforehand and allow the prayers' words and the experience to penetrate your inner being. Pay attention to each liturgical lesson — whether it is the reference to G-d's kingship that reminds you that everything and every moment was created for no other purpose but to serve Him; or the *shofar* of the *Akeidah* that represents the unlimited love that our ancestors had for G-d. Listen to the words the rabbi has to say, learn the texts that accentuate the themes of these days, and make mental notes of whatever drives you to draw closer to G-d. Then, right after *Havdalah,* take out your notepad and jot down your thoughts. Don't worry about being coherent, and don't pay attention to grammar or style. Just get the ideas down. We'll use those notes when we meet next time."

He had already begun retreating toward his home when he noted my look of confusion. I had to admit that the words "Keep your mind present" and "empty yourself out to allow the experience to penetrate your inner being" sounded so profound, but that I did not really know what he meant by them.

"Perhaps an analogy is in order..." he began, as he settled into the passenger's seat. "Imagine that you are on a family trip to Massada that you've been anticipating for a long time. Your friends have told you that the sunrise from the mountain's peak is breathtaking and that you should be sure to get there in time to see it.

"So you all arrive at the foot of the mountain, very excited. The morning rays have already begun to emerge from beyond the horizon. There are but a few moments before the sun will surface. As you reach the peak, you grab your camera. You get into position and gently rest your finger on the shutter button, anxiously awaiting that special moment. And then it happens. The sun breaks through the horizon and, in an instant, you press — but to no avail. You press again, and again no luck. You look at the camera and, in horror, notice that your batteries are drained! Panic sets in. You had been planning and talking about this moment for months. You desperately search your bag for spare batteries, but it's empty. You ask your wife, your children. You ask the people to your left and the people to your right. Everyone joins in the search.

"Finally, you hear the words, 'Here! I found them!' You look up to the sky as you stretch out your hand. The sun has nearly cleared the horizon. There is little time left. You fumble in your haste, but manage to load the camera. You take aim, snap, and click — the picture is taken! Yes, you got it! You caught the sunrise... or did you?"

I did not respond, so he continued reflectively. "Of course, it all depends on what it means to 'catch the sunrise.' If it means getting a picture that you can store, then yes, you got it. But if it means experiencing the sunrise in such a way that its beauty inspires and touches the core of your inner being, that it stirs your heart till it's bursting with awe at the wonders of G-d's world, then I'm afraid that you've missed it. Why? Because you cannot rely on an external device in order to absorb this kind of majestic moment. You must take it in and experience it with all of your senses. In other words, you must be fully present in the moment.

"Of course, an encounter with G-d, especially on these holiest of days — days He is most accessible to us — is more spectacular than any scenery we will ever witness. It should evoke more passion than do any of His handiworks. It is an experience in which you must immerse your whole self, you must stay fully present."

"And emptying myself out...?" I asked.

"Literally empty yourself of your predispositions — your thoughts and feelings — so that you can be a vessel to receive G-d's influence. That is how you can achieve the highest levels of connection."

"Connection...?" I persisted.

"I think you have enough to begin your journey. As you will soon learn, connection — like a hearty piece of chocolate cake — cannot be fully understood and appreciated until it is tasted. Experience Rosh Hashanah as we have described. Afterwards, we will be able to discuss these matters more intelligently."

And with that, my mentor extended to me his greetings for a good year and walked back to his home.

STEP 1

A Framework for Change

MY MEETING WITH MY mentor was as inspirational as it was informative. I came away very motivated to do things differently this year and felt fully focused going into Rosh Hashanah. It's hard to describe the passion that was welling within me since leaving his home. All I can say is that I could not wait to take on these "days of awe."

Now one of my most inspiring Rosh Hashanahs has just ended and I am dutifully doing my homework, writing down the moments and messages that moved me most over the last two days. I realize that there is something paradoxical to the sentence I just wrote. After all, *inspiring* and *dutifully*, and especially the word homework, do not seem to go together! But it *does* feel like I am doing homework; I had to make a conscious effort to seat myself at my desk and follow through. The reality of this moment sure looks different than what I had envisioned it to be just a few hours ago. In *shul*, I had no doubts that my uplifted soul would allow the words to flow in magnificent prose. Instead, I had to unceremoniously *schlep* myself here and remind myself that if I do not write anything down, there might be unbearable consequences: My mentor would be very disappointed with me, and worse yet, I might repeat last year's miserable *Ne'ilah* experience...

Well, I'm here now, and these are some of my reflections from the last two days. They are not necessarily novel and insightful ideas, because that was not the assignment. Instead, they are merely observations about myself, and messages that managed to penetrate my outer layers of consciousness since the start of these awesome days...

FIRST OF ALL, my mentor's parting thought about staying present for the prayers created a breakthrough I never would have anticipated. For one thing, I did not once look ahead to see how many pages were left to pray. I did not check the time. I just stayed with each prayer as it appeared. I stayed staunchly in the present, and permitted myself to bathe in each and every moment.

But there was more to the presence that I gave to the prayers. Trying to follow his suggestion to "empty myself out," I set aside my distracting thoughts and feelings in order to allow myself to be moved by the words, the melodies, and the whole experience.

To be honest, I was still not sure how to do that. So I experimented. I tried taking a few deep breaths, relaxing my body, closing my eyes, swaying gently, and allowing intrusive thoughts to ease their way out of my mind rather than fighting them. I must have succeeded to some extent, because—to use his metaphor—I tasted the cake called "connection!" And I must say that it was delicious.

In the past, I would have moments of despair; from time to time, my wandering mind would remind me that it was Rosh Hashanah and demand that my heart muster intention. Then, when my heart would resist, my mind would command my body to *shuckle*—very, very hard—with the hope that activity would somehow jumpstart my soul.

BUT THIS TIME, I hardly had such moments. This time, genuine intensity came through immersion in the moment, and my heart was captivated. It had no interest in being anywhere else. I finally discovered my spiritual taste buds: those dry and stale words that I had mouthed for many years suddenly had a delectable taste and fragrant smell; they had a soft touch and a sweet sound. I found reassurance, security, safety and love as I stepped into each phrase, places that I had no mind or heart to leave. I was in the zone!

This, I now know, is what my mentor meant. And it was an extraordinary experience. I felt that I had been transformed.

As I reflect on these words, I'm surprised by my poetic flair! I never talk that way. But then again, I never really felt that way. I suspect that my new awareness has given rise to a new vocabulary, and I don't mind it one bit.

So here are the thoughts — the honest insights — that moved me over the past 48 hours. I guess you can call this — reflecting on the thoughts that will form the framework for *teshuvah* — **Step 1** of my mentor's plan.

1. These past few years have been very unsettling for humanity in general, and Jews in Israel in particular. The majority of people — including me — have been searching for support and security in a turbulent and dangerous world. But while so many people are trying to reassure us — governments speaking to their citizens, parents to their children, airlines to their passengers — deep down we know that no one can *really* guarantee anyone else's well-being. Today's realities have made it clear that there is no other source of support and security than G-d Himself. Of course, we Jews have always believed this. But, I'm a bit embarrassed to admit that this truth — as reality — did not hit home for me until I read it last night in the psalm starting with the words "*L'David Hashem Ori...*" With my newfound "in the moment" awareness, I saw that the entire paragraph, even without commentary, is the reassurance that our entire generation so desperately needs. "G-d is my light and my salvation, whom shall I fear? G-d is my life's strength, whom shall I dread?" I was touched.

The plain, simple reading of these words resonated so well with me that I chose to make them my theme for these days. The frame for my impending *teshuvah*, my "*Ana Hashem — Please G-d*," would be formed by the simple, yet profound reality that G-d is my sole source of support and security.

2. One good thing leads to another. Drawn by *L'Dovid's* opening words, I discovered a gem in a later line. King David says, "Even when my parents forsake me, G-d is there." At first, I could not relate to this verse, to children forsaken by their parents. But then I remembered a story: A young daughter of a venerated rabbi told her father that she was afraid of G-d and His judgments on Rosh Hashanah. The rabbi thought for a moment, and then asked her whether or not she thought he loved her. Of course he did, very much, and she agreed. "Then," he continued, "Remember, at all times, that G-d loves you a million times more than I ever could!"

   That message struck a chord in me — that while parents love their children, G-d loves them even more. And that image, of the boundlessly loving Father, is one that I focused on throughout the two days.

3. I came across a thought from the Rebbe of Kotzk that deeply influenced my *shofar* experience: The Kotzker had been approached by a *Chasid* who wanted a blessing for wealth. He responded with a story: A king and

his son had a falling out, and the prince was banished from the palace. Years later, after living in poverty and filth, the prince was approached by his father's minister with a royal deal—any one wish would be granted. "I would like new clothes to replace my ragged ones," he humbly requested; whereupon the minister said, "You fool! You could have asked to be brought back to the palace in the king's good graces and you would have had all that you want—including new clothes!" The Kotzker's point, of course, was that the focus of our prayers should be to reconnect to G-d—to go home to our Father—for once we do that, all blessings will come our way, including wealth. I allowed this idea to permeate my mind as I listened to the *shofar*. It was not a time to think of any one particular request, but to submit my entire self to G-d.

4. I am amazed at how deeply affected I was by passages that I normally rattle off every day. For instance, yesterday, as I read the account of the *Akeidah,* I was blown away by its essential message—that nothing in life, not even our children, has any meaning unless it is defined within the context of our relationship with G-d. Our forefather Avraham dramatically demonstrated that we cannot withhold anything from G-d, because, in reality, nothing exists outside of Him. Everything is His and He is everything. I spent some time trying to assimilate this teaching so that each time we would affirm G-d's

sovereignty, I would be reminded of its far-reaching implications.

There! That should do for now. It's getting late. I have been writing for twenty minutes, an eternity when there are so many things to do.

As I sit back in my chair and look over the pages that I had just written, I am amazed — not so much by the quality of my thoughts but by the sheer volume of words that I had written.

You see, all beginnings are hard, but when they involve writing, they are doubly difficult for me. So as soon as I heard that the plan required writing, a part of me had already checked out. "This is not for me. There's no way I'll be able to discipline myself to do this," I thought.

And what's worse, my despair was reinforced by an awareness that many other people would react with the same resistance. I really thought I'd stand no chance.

But somehow I came through, though I'm not sure how. I just did it! And what's most amazing to me is that once I pushed myself to write the first few words, the rest flowed. Looking back at it now, I can honestly say that it wasn't so hard, and that I no longer feel faint at the thought of my mentor giving me more writing assignments.

If this journey ultimately leads to real change, then this early success may yet prove to be a critical turning point in that process...

STEP 1: Create the framework.

STRATEGIES: Reflect... connect...and ask yourself:

- *Why is my relationship with G-d important to me?*
- *What thoughts make me feel impelled to return to Him?*

STEP 2

The Vision That Leads to Success

TODAY WAS THE *Fast of Gedaliah* which, of course means, no food and extra prayers. As a rule, I do not fast well. In fact, it's as big of a challenge for me to miss one meal as it is for others to miss all three. So my expectations for the day were pretty low. But, to my surprise, things were different — very different. Today my mind was focused on more important matters than food. To be sure, I had a hunger; but it was not for toast or juice — it was for something much more salient and spiritual.

I craved to talk to G-d!

There are two reasons for why I considered this strange: First (and again — forgive me for being too honest, but this is, after all, a personal journal), that I had such a great desire to pray, an actual longing that was with me the moment I awoke; and second, that the inspiration of Rosh Hashanah seemed to carry over all the way into the next day.

When I shared these thoughts with my mentor at our afternoon meeting, he was not at all surprised. At first, he assumed that my inspiration had greater strength and substance to continue for another day because I had taken the time to record my Rosh Hashanah reflections the night before. That made me especially glad that I had pushed myself to do it.

But then he looked me in the eye and, after a brief silence, beamed with a mentor's *nachas*: "You were present!"

For a few more moments, neither of us spoke. Yes, I *had* been present. I already knew that. And even if I had not known exactly what my mentor had meant the other day when he first sprung that word on me, I knew it now as I was experiencing *his* presence with *me* — with his eye contact, interest, and all.

"How did you know?" I asked.

"Because when you are present, you connect... and that connection lasts."

HE LET ME contemplate those words — "connection lasts" — while they echoed in my mind. That was his way: he would let me mull over my thoughts and savor their insights, without rushing to the next point. And then, with confidence, he assured me that I would continue to discover and experience the truth of these words as my process of *teshuvah* continued.

But he was also an exceptionally perceptive man. He saw the words "why?" and "how?" written all over my face. He sensed, as he did at our first meeting, that I really needed to hear more. And though he was a man of few words, he knew not to leave a man like me hanging with uncertainty.

So he gently held my arm and walked with me to a nearby sofa. And as we both settled in, my mentor began: "I am sure that you will agree that we have both come a long way since infancy."

I nodded in obvious agreement, though I had no idea where he was going with that obscure statement.

"Back when we were infants, we enjoyed a life without complexities. That is because we lacked what psychologists call "object-permanence." During that time, nothing had an absolute existence. Instead, it was our field of view that literally defined our entire reality. As soon as we saw a toy, it became part of our world, and we may well have cried or tried to reach for it. But the moment it was taken out of our sight, we went on with life as though the toy had never existed. And that was true with the people in our lives as well — we celebrated when our mothers entered our field of view, and grieved when they left it. In short, we lived in the here and now, holding onto one object, one person, and one experience at a time.

"But, as we matured, we began to recognize that life is

way more complex than that. As adults, we can and must hold on to many things at once. Spouses and children, friends and colleagues, jobs, and chores all coexist within our one intricate reality and they all need to be juggled. And that, as you know, is not easy."

At this point, my perfunctory nod turned thoughtful and passionate. I certainly knew what he meant when he spoke of the challenges of living with object-permanence! How easy life would be if we only had to deal with one reality at a time. The thought seduced me into a relaxed, contemplative position when I quickly realized that my mentor had not yet finished his thought—and I still was not quite sure where he was heading. So I straightened up and motioned for more.

"But while object-permanence makes life complex, it also allows for meaningful relationships, ones that can transcend time and space. You see, whereas a baby can only love and relate to what he sees, an adult can be in relationships no matter where he is because he has the ability to hold those who he cherishes within his reality even when they are out of view. And that is what *you* have achieved with G-d. You have, so to speak, kept Him in your reality even beyond those moments when you were actively connecting with Him."

"You mean through my prayers?" I asked.

"...And through your work towards *teshuvah,*" he added.

"But how long does this object-permanence last? How long can we keep others within our reality when they are out of our view?" I asked.

"That depends on the quality of connection. Look at Yaakov and Yosef in *Breishis*. The commentaries explain that 'These are the generations of Yaakov:Yosef...' teaches that there was a profound connection between them. This explains how — when Yosef found himself on the verge of sin with the daughter of Potiphar, years after he had left his home — his father's image appeared before him. The depth of their connection enabled Yosef to hold his father in his reality for many years."

And then, in a confident tone, my mentor concluded:

"You, my friend, will continue to learn a lot more during these next few days about the power of connection. You have already had the experience of holding on to G-d for a day, and that, you say, has been an unusually pleasant experience. May you continue to deepen your connection — through prayer and repentance — so that wherever life takes you, you will find yourself always walking with G-d..."

As I whispered "amen," he had already switched gears and was ready for today's assignment.

"AT THIS POINT, I like to formally frame the process of change by formulating what I call 'a global desire.'"

"But weren't these reflections the frame?" I asked him, as I lifted yesterday's homework.

"They are the basis for it. And because you diligently did your work last night, today's assignment will be both easier and have greater substance."

I gave myself a mental pat on the back. After all, it's not often I'm praised for being diligent.

"A global desire is "the big picture," a goal that is painted with broad strokes. It is the vision you have for your *whole* relationship with G-d as you want it to be. Do not be concerned, at first, about the steps you will need to take to bring this vision to fruition. And do not be discouraged if you feel you are far from the goal you want to achieve. For now, think big, and just describe your dream relationship with G-d. Remember to keep it personal and speak directly to Him in whatever words are meaningful to you — as you should with everything you put into your script for *teshuvah*."

As I looked over my written reflections, I wondered how I would convert them into global desires. Then I noticed some key operative words and whispered them aloud: "Safety, security, love... I want to love G-d..."

"When? In what circumstances?" my mentor prodded.

"All the time, in all circumstances," I answered.

"Then put it in those terms."

"I want to love G-d all the time."

"That's it! And when you have fully described the desire, in vivid detail, indicate that this is what frames the *teshuvah* that you are about to do. Make it clear that the steps you will take in correcting your past misdeeds are not for personal empowerment but, rather, to lead you to the desire you have described."

And to complete the point, he explained:

"There are many people who think a single, isolated behavior change, on its own, is all that is needed to get through these times. But if there is no big picture — a context where that random behavior change fits — it will hardly take them anywhere. It's like walking eastward on a westbound train, we get nowhere fast.

"No, we must start with an aspiration, and only then commit to specific steps that, one at a time, will take us towards that vision." And on that note, we walked towards the door.

"Keep in mind," he added, "that whether or not you are successful in achieving your goals depends largely on how well the global vision reflects your innermost drive. That's why your work must be yours. Stay away from clichés and make sure to use your own thoughts and language. Give it lots of thought and feeling. And, whatever you come up with, make sure to say it like you mean it, because that is the only way that it will work."

STEP 2: Formulate a global desire, your vision for success.

STRATEGIES: Be real... and ask yourself:

- *How would you characterize your dream relationship with G-d?*
- *How would achieving that vision affect your life? How would you think differently?*
- *How would you act differently? How would you feel differently?*

STEP 3

Taking Stock

I WOKE UP THIS MORNING unsure about whether or not I would return to my mentor. Not that I am dissatisfied with his plan. Just the opposite — it's working too well! Here I am, on the third step of a ten-step plan, and I already feel that I have achieved my goal: G-d is my confidant — though just a few days ago, that seemed so impossible. Yet here I am, in love with G-d, thinking about Him at all times, saying my prayers with incredible conviction, and trying to emulate His ways when dealing with the people in my life. I feel pity for those who do not experience life the way I am experiencing it. And so, feeling that I have reached the peak of my growth, I thought to drop a thank you note in my mentor's mailbox and leave him alone.

I wrestled with this uncertainty throughout my drive to his house. I concocted so many excuses for why it was the perfect time to pack it up and bid him farewell. I even argued that it was wrong for me to take more of his time.

"He must be busy with his own preparations for *teshuvah*," I thought to myself. "If I have more to gain from him, I ought to wait until after Yom Kippur to continue. For now, I will complete the work on my own and make a *real* commitment to call him *right* away, even before I break my fast."

AS I PARKED the car, I sat for a few more contemplative moments. "Those words sound so familiar," I reminisced. And then it hit me! I began to smile, and soon I found myself chuckling. Here I am, standing in full view of the "Promised Land" that I yearned to reach, and my mind is still recycling the same nonsense that almost kept me from calling my mentor in the first place. And, what's worse, is that it's having the same effect! How could this be, after all the work I've done?

I began to suspect that maybe I hadn't reached my goal, after all. I mean, how could it be this easy? I never even broke a sweat! Had I been fooling myself to think that conjuring a deeper love for G-d was enough and that it would be permanent? Was this illusion just a form of procrastination, some kind of inner mechanism preventing me from really digging into the job at hand?

With that thought, I managed to make my way out of the car, and left my *procrastinating self* with all of its uncertainties behind. And as I walked towards the front door, I felt as though I had walked away from a part of myself that I was wholly determined to defeat.

With that, I knocked on the door with a purpose. After our usual greetings, my mentor began the next round.

"So, how did you manage with formulating a global desire?"

I paused. I was not sure whether to open up and share my morning struggles with him. In the end, I decided I would not. There was no purpose, I thought, to revisit that experience. I had dealt with it and was feeling ready to move on. Besides, I felt too empowered by the confident and assertive state I was in to put it into jeopardy.

"I did the work," I said, as I flashed my homework, "and I'm ready for more."

I was sure that he would perceive the scars from my inner battle, and that they would arouse his curiosity. I was prepared for his questions, but they did not come. Instead, without skipping a beat, he reached for today's assignment.

"HERE," HE SAID, as he reached for several sheets of paper. They were copies of the *"Al Chet" Viduy,* the standard Yom Kippur Confession taken from the *machzor.* "Our rabbis have provided us with a list of transgressions for us to confess: its purpose is to satisfy the requirement to detail our wrongdoings."

Of course, I was familiar with it. Once again, my mentor was living up to his claim that his plan was based on our literature. But how was he going to use this list?

"Now, this list contains generic and general statements, so to make it more personal, we must *chunk down!*"

I gave him a quizzical look. *That* term did not sound very Talmudic, to say the least. But he was quick to elaborate.

"Look at some of the behaviors for which we ask forgiveness: 'Having a hardened heart... Insufficient respect for parents... Corrupt business dealings...' These are all behaviors that everyone can relate to, but not necessarily in the same way. After all, what do they *really* mean — *specifically*?"

He paused to collect his thoughts, and then continued.

"You see, G-d requires us to take responsibility for many areas of life, and each one has a whole range of ways it can be upheld or violated. For instance, to the unrefined person, 'do not murder' means just that: Do not put a bullet through someone's head. But 'do not murder' remains relevant even to a person who would never consider such a thing; only it has a more sublime meaning, a derivative mandate such as not to embarrass others. So, when these two people confess their respective acts of murder, though they speak the same words, they mean very different things."

And then he summarized:

"'**Chunking down**' means to tailor these broad-stroked statements to our lives by making them more personal and specific. And we do that by simply asking ourselves, '*How specifically,* did I violate each transgression?' and then promptly pencil it in.

I looked at the familiar list, but it never seemed as formidable as it did now. "I need to personalize them all?"

"Do at least one before we meet again. But the more you are able to do—and for that you must know your own stamina—the more material you will have to work with later."

Relieved, I took the sheets and looked them over. I had no further questions; it seemed simple enough. And so, seeing that I was content, he stood up to escort me out.

BUT MY BODY weighed heavily and I stayed seated. I needed to find out what would have happened had I not returned today. So, while preserving my self-imposed code of silence concerning my inner battle, I asked him whether what we had done to date could, "theoretically," stand on its own.

"That is an excellent question. In fact, this may be a good time to talk about the distinction between *teshuvah* and *kaparah*."

I leaned back into my chair while he continued.

"On the one hand we know that there is a structure to doing *teshuvah*. We saw some steps in the Rambam, and there are many more in classical works, such as *Shaarei*

Teshuvah. Yet at the same time, the Talmud says that if a person who is a known sinner proposes to a woman on condition that he is perfectly righteous, we have to consider the possibility that he had the stirrings of *teshuvah* in his heart that could make him righteous, and his proposal legitimate. Now, let me ask you: How is it possible for a person, in a moment's time and only in his heart, to satisfy all the steps of *teshuvah* — to be considered perfectly righteous?"

I straightened up, awaiting the answer.

"It is clear that there are levels to *teshuvah.* The first, which is what we have done to date, is to reconnect with G-d. And that is primarily a matter of orientation. It doesn't require a formal structure. It *can* be done in a moment's time, and in the heart. And don't be fooled by its simplicity, because its effects are enormous. The Rambam (*Teshuvah,* 7:7) describes how radically one's quality of life is improved once he has positioned himself in connection with G-d: "He calls out to G-d and is answered immediately... he fulfills *mitzvos* and they are accepted with pleasure and with joy..."

"And then, there is *kaparah,* the process by which one wipes clean the slate he has dirtied with his sins, and undoes the damage caused by them. Cleansing requires time and effort. It demands confession, regret, and the rest of the steps of *teshuvah.* And while we all want *kaparah* — to answer your question, an important level of *teshuvah* can be achieved without it.

"This is important for people to know. Otherwise, if they think that *teshuvah* with *kaparah* is an all-or-nothing deal, they can quickly get overwhelmed and discouraged. People need the reassurance that the first level of *teshuvah*, which is so accessible to all, is a great accomplishment and can be achieved on its own. Everyone can find this moment: when your heart experiences the inner stirrings of *teshuvah* that can make you righteous.

"So, it seems that you have reached a milestone in the *teshuvah* process. You have reconnected. I am not the authority to measure your work, but in my humble opinion, you could have called it quits and still have achieved great things."

Though I gave way to a smile, I contained my celebration within. I sensed that this was a big moment for me.

But as I closed my eyes and pondered his point, my smile grew bigger. I reminded myself of a thought I had during that fateful *Ne'ilah* experience last year. At the time, I prayed that G-d grant me "an extension for *teshuvah*" for I felt I had nothing yet to show for myself. But, based on what we just discussed, I really *did* have what to show. I had the "stirrings" of *teshuvah* that can turn on a dime, and that — as the Talmud says — could have given me the status of a *ba'al teshuvah* with all of the benefits described by the Rambam. Sure, I might have needed the extension for *kaparah*... but the *teshuvah* was there! What a discovery!

But I kept it all to myself. That whole inner dialogue from last year's *Ne'ilah* was terribly embarrassing and I was not going to share it with anyone, not even my mentor.

As if to keep me from getting complacent, my mentor rolled right on: "But with today's work we are setting our sights on even greater heights. By taking inventory of our misdeeds, we begin a journey that leads us towards higher levels of *teshuvah*. G-d willing, with diligence and discipline, we can move from connection with G-d to *kaparah*."

"Amen."

STEP 3: Take stock.

STRATEGIES: Survey the Yom Kippur *Viduy* list and "chunk down."

For each one, ask yourself:

"How have I been vulnerable to...(specific transgression)?"

STEP 4

Regret That Is Useful

I RETURNED TO MY MENTOR with my list in hand. I had marked it up considerably, humbling myself from the smug satisfaction I had experienced only a day before.

"How can I possibly address all of my misdeeds?" I complained, as I showed him my work. "Did I mark off too many?"

He did not respond, so I reworded my challenge.

"I've always been told that we should take on one behavior at a time when doing *teshuvah*. But at that pace and with this long list, how many lifetimes would it take for me to fix myself?" I cut myself short. My frustration was getting the best of me.

But my mentor was prepared. He took the list from my hand and, after giving it a quick look, quietly commented:

"You did your homework. You're staying the course. I am impressed."

Then he placed it face down on the table and said, "Remind me, please, how did you manage with the global desire?"

I was caught of guard. Emotionally, I was in a very different place today.

"Well, it went well, I thought."

"Meaning?" he persisted.

"It went so well that I was surprised at how close I was to achieving my goal. All I did was to describe it and put it into words, and the whole day yesterday, I felt like I had reached the finish line. I felt like I was already a changed person. I'm embarrassed to tell you this," I said, lowering my voice, "I even thought of not coming back to you till after Yom Kippur."

"And today?"

"To be honest, today I am a little discouraged. I don't believe that a true confidant of G-d scores this badly," I said, pointing to the list. "And if I knew this was all in the past, I could tolerate it. But even with all the love towards G-d that I felt yesterday, I cannot imagine fixing all of these anytime in the near future."

"So the contrast between these two days has been very alarming for you," he noted.

"To say the least," I answered.

"Well, it makes a lot of sense. I mean, you are trying to

step into being a confidant of G-d while housing so many skeletons in your closet. I imagine it makes you feel... hypocritical?"

"You got it!" I confirmed.

"LET ME CAPTURE the moment and talk about today's assignment. It's about regret—and it sounds to me like you are well into it. Structurally, I like to revisit my list and put some of my misgivings on paper. I may include regrets related to the consequences of the specific behaviors I listed. For example, it may be that, by saying certain hurtful words, I caused someone to lose his job. So I will write that down. And I will also write what embarrasses me about being the cause of that person's pain. But I also make sure to put special emphasis on the regrets I have with regards to how these behaviors distanced me from the global desire I myself so carefully constructed. In your case," he said, perusing my list, "write a few words explaining how 'eating without making the proper blessings' has kept you from loving G-d the way you know you should."

I ventured, "Like not acknowledging the love G-d has for me by providing me with all of my needs?"

"That's the idea. And, as with the rest of the work, flesh it out. Write two or three sentences expressing your remorse."

"I should have no problem with that. It will just take some time."

"Yes," he agreed, "time is of the essence. Just make sure you do at least one, with an openness to do others."

At that point, my mentor could see that I needed reassurance.

"THERE ARE TWO points you need to consider whenever you begin to feel overwhelmed by this list. First, there is real cause for concern only if you present yourself to G-d as a 'finished product,' despite your lengthy list of flaws. But when you present yourself as a work-in-progress, it is altogether different. You see, there is an important distinction between the two. Let me describe this with an analogy.

"An exuberant father took his young son to buy him his first bicycle. It would be a used one, in need of many minor repairs, but the storeowner assured him that he would make it as good as new. The father agreed, and the storeowner raised the bike on a lift and began to work. Now remember, this was an exuberant father who wanted the best for his little lad. While the storeowner was working on the brakes, the father noticed another problem and said, 'The back wheel is slightly bent.'

"'I'll get to it soon, sir,' replied the storeowner, his attention still focused on the disabled brakes.

"The father breathed a sigh of relief knowing that it could be fixed. While the storeowner was working on the back wheel, the father noticed that a part was missing from the gears, and he pointed that out too.

"'I'll get to it soon, sir,' replied the storeowner, his attention still focused on the back wheel.

"The father, again, breathed a sigh of relief. And, once again, when, while the storeowner was working on the gears, the father noticed another problem, and said:

"'I'm really sorry, but the front tire is flat.'

"This time, the storeowner turned his attention away from the bike and squarely faced the father.

"'Sir, we both know there is a lot of work to be done on this bike. We also both know that you will not pay for it until all the work is done. So, I ask you, please wait with your questions until I put down my tools, and present the bike as a final product. In the meantime, take a seat in the waiting area and let me do my work.'"

My mentor paused before applying the lesson.

"We, too, must see ourselves as a work-in-progress. We cannot expect to fix our brakes and gears and wheels in one twist of a wrench. But we must begin somewhere. And as long as we do not present ourselves as a finished product, we can ask G-d to extend His patience while we take the time we need to make all the repairs."

"'A work-in-progress'... Brilliant, and very encouraging," I thought aloud as I tried to assimilate the concept into my experience, "even though I know it means that the work never ends. There's no point in time when I'll be 'a finished product.'"

My mentor affirmed with a simple nod.

"The key is to keep moving forward, one repair at a time."

His nod continued.

"And the second point?" I asked.

He gently placed his hand on my shoulder. "Let's save that for next time." And with that, he adjourned our meeting for the day.

STEP 4: Use regret constructively.

STRATEGIES: Ask yourself:

- *Why is it so bad to violate G-d's will, in general?*
- *Why do I feel bad for having committed____ (specific sin or wrongdoing)?*
- *How did it pull me down?*
- *Did it cause damage to others?*
- *In what way has this (specific sin) kept me from achieving my global desire?*

STEPS 5, 6, 7

Three Strategies to Hit the Target

TODAY WE BEGAN THE final stretch. My mentor told me that we would spend the rest of our time developing a thought-out, tailor-made resolution that can, with G-d's help, stand the test of time, and that we would begin with three closely related steps — 5, 6, and 7. I rolled up my sleeves and accepted the charge.

But before we started, my mentor took out time to recognize my efforts, pointing out that the process of planning change is critical.

"It is evident, from the excitement — and anxiety — that you bring with you to our sessions, that you are taking this work to heart. That is so important, because the whole planning process of *teshuvah* is as critical as the resolution that it leads you to make."

Then he paused to collect his thoughts. It was clear

that he was trying hard to present the next point without the risk of it being misinterpreted. He closed his eyes for a few seconds, and then continued, "The process of change is tough," he began. "It takes time and energy to reflect and resolve, as you are seeing for yourself. Modern life does not readily accommodate that kind of work. Because of that, many well-meaning and fully observant Jews coast through life without attempting serious changes.

"Sometimes, during the Yom Kippur season, for instance, they realize that they want to change. They want to be different, but they're not ready to do all the work. So they look for pre-packaged solutions. You will hear them say things like, 'I heard that this righteous person accepted upon himself to pray with a *siddur* this year. If that is good enough for him, it is certainly good enough for me.'

"I've had times myself when I desperately reached for a one-size-fits-all solution. But it was far from ideal. Without the struggles and investment of effort, the commitment lacked meaning and, in most cases, simply did not fit. Of course, as you can imagine, it usually did not last."

And after a short pause to be sure I was with him, he summarized his point with one simple sentence: "When it comes to personal growth, the journey itself is a destination!"

With that introduction, my mentor went on to detail the day's work.

"LOOK BACK ON your global desire and your list of shortcomings. Use them as resources to help you identify one specific area on which you will focus your growth for the year. That way, you will repair a misdeed of the past and move in the direction of your deepest desire. You may want to improve in your relations with the members of your family, learn better, deal more honestly in business. The choice is yours. And write this commitment on a separate piece of paper."

I wrote down his examples.

"Now, it's true that everyone can improve in every area of Jewish life. That's why it is so easy to convince ourselves that the "resolution of the day" — someone else's resolution — is as relevant to us as it is to the one who made it, and bypass the work we are doing here. But for growth to be meaningful and lasting, it needs to be incremental, going from where we are one day to where we need to be the next. Taking on someone else's commitment is completely random, as it pays no attention to the greater context of where *you* are holding in life.

"So we need to rally every ounce of wisdom and self-awareness, and determine what potential changes fall within the range of *our* personal *growth edge*, and *that* should be the focus of our resolutions."

"Growth edge..." That was a new term for me. I let him elaborate, as he showed no signs of slowing down.

"What is a growth edge, you ask?" He had read my mind.

"Well, just imagine you are positioned on a growth ladder. Below you are rungs representing all of life's challenges that you have already mastered; above you are rungs you have yet to master. The next rung up is where your next agenda lies. That is your 'growth edge,' and therein lie the roots of your resolution. Developmentally speaking, that is your next step.

"BUT HOW CAN I identify that?"

"What behavior will open up a new frontier for you? What behavior have you been unable to master and, as a result, has held you back from going to the next level? These are the questions you have to ask yourself as you look at your list of shortcomings. In short, you are looking for a *difference that makes the difference* in your life — where you are, today."

"Can you give me an example?"

He thought for a moment, and then suggested, "I may very well need to work on my laziness. But if I am in a deep struggle with my marriage, I need to find the quality that I lack that will improve my relationship with my wife and get working on it. To whatever extent that problem causes everything else to suffer, it becomes my priority. That will be the difference that makes a great big difference. With that knowledge, I will have found my growth edge.

"The stakes of misjudging your growth edge can be great," he cautioned. "King Solomon warns that 'the foolishness of man will turn him off the path, and his heart will become angry with G-d,' which the Gaon of Vilna applies to a man who, in his quest to grow, overextends himself. Such a person is certain to fail and, in his frustration, will blame G-d for that failure."

"Then what do you suggest?" I asked, revealing some concern in my tone.

"That's what friends are for!" he replied, matter-of-factly. "It's not easy to make self-assessments of this nature when there are so many internal influences that can skew our judgment. In fact, self-development comes from being aware of what others know about you but that you don't even know about yourself. So the best advice I have for you is to follow the words of the *Mishnah*: 'Acquire a friend for yourself.' The commentaries point out that among the most profound benefits of acquiring a good friendship is gaining a comrade for growth. Talk to a friend, in confidence, and let him help you explore your personal growth edge. And, you can do the same for him. You will benefit from each other's insight, as well as the mutual support you give one another in your efforts to make lasting changes in your lives."

"But can't you share your wisdom to help me find my growth edge?" I persisted.

"Whether I am 'wise' or not is not the issue; the advantage of a friend is that he knows you and, if he cares enough about you, he will respond openly to your request to help you in your self-discovery. And, as I said before, you can be there for him as well.

"Now here is the challenge. We have to convert this broad-stroked goal to one that is concrete and unambiguous. Simply saying that you will be patient, for example, is not enough. Instead, you need to ask yourself, 'What will I do, *specifically*, that will demonstrate patience?'"

When I asked him how this is done, he turned to *me* as the expert. But I dropped the ball.

"WHY NOT START with a strategy you have already used?" he suggested. "After all, you knew what to do when you wanted to learn how to do *teshuvah*. You came to me because you thought I had a plan that might work for you. In the same way, search for someone who is the living embodiment of your personal vision and find out how he does it. Observe him; ask him questions; and then do what he does. It is as simple as that."

I thought of a few people I know, and what their reactions would be if I asked them for that kind of guidance. "What if he doesn't know how he does it?" I asked.

"That's a good question. After all, some people are great at what they do without knowing how they do it. But even if they are unaware of their strategies, they still have them. So you will need to ask the right questions in order to help you, and him, reveal those strategies. Find out what he does, specifically, when he is acting in the way you would like to act.

"For example, let's say you're trying to improve your capacity for empathy, and your friend seems to care so much about the experiences of other people. Ask him how he reacts, for instance, when someone shares a personal problem with him. What does he say? How does he stand? How does he breathe? What is his tone? Where does he look? Questions like that. You want to be so specific that you can actually emulate his way of being by stepping into the posture that makes it happen. And to do that, you need a detailed description of what that posture looks like.

"Remember, you are searching for behaviors — for those actions will form the basis of your practical commitment. But your greatest find will be when you elicit from your expert the mindset you need to make that happen. Find out what thoughts he thinks and what perspective he maintains when he demonstrates the qualities you're trying to emulate. Check to see whether he has some sort of guiding philosophy that helps him along. After all, effective thoughts produce effective feelings, which, in turn, produce effective behavior. And you need to adopt those attitudes, with their specific words, in order to make meaningful and sustained changes in your life."

HE WINKED, AS he added, "And in your search for experts, don't overlook your own expertise..."

I looked at him quizzically.

"Just because you aspire to be, say, more diligent in your studies, and you search for someone whose strength is diligence, it doesn't mean that *you* have never been diligent yourself. It may have been an uncommon experience, but I am sure it has happened. Think back to such a time, and tap into the thoughts and behaviors *you* used as your strategies. When you use your own successes as a standard, and work towards reproducing them on a more consistent basis, you will feel more confident that you can achieve it. You've done it before and you can do it again! Emulating yourself makes it more realistic and increases your chances of success.

"In fact, I always thought that one reason why our rabbis require that we step up our commitments during *Aseres Y'mei Teshuvah,* observing stringencies we do not normally keep the rest of the year, is to have us role model righteousness for ourselves. In this way, our aspirations are for a standard that we ourselves have set. Having done it before, even if only for a week, makes us feel that it can be relevant to our lives. It gets us to think, 'Hey, if I did it for a week, why couldn't I do it for longer?'"

My mentor had more to say, but felt that it was more than enough work for one day. For now, he wanted me to go out and learn from the experts in the field of my choice — including myself.

STEP 5: **Find your growth edge.**

STRATEGIES: **Consult a friend... and ask yourself:**

- *What new way of being will open up a new frontier for me?*
- *What thought or behavior has held me back from going to my next level of growth?*
- *Have people complained about a particular shortcoming of mine?*
- *What kind of personal change in my way of being will be the difference that makes the difference?*

STEP 6: **Find effective thoughts and attitudes.**

STRATEGIES: **Ask your role model (and/or yourself):**

- *What goes through your mind when you do the desired (specific) behavior?*
- *What thoughts get you to do (the behavior)?*
- *What is important about (the behavior)?*

STEP 7: **Identify target behaviors.**

STRATEGIES: **Ask your role model (and/or yourself):**

- *What specifically do you do when you are successfully doing ___ (the behavior)?*
- *How do you breathe? How do you move? How do you stand? What do you say?*

STEP 8

A Personal Success Card

AS I STARTED FEELING confident that a practical change could occur in my life, I reread my list of shortcomings carefully to find a really important area to work on myself. Without getting into the details of how I made my choice, I determined that I would work on controlling my strong reactions. Now, it's not like I'm a loose cannon, firing away at all hours of the day and night; but when I get triggered, I lose myself more than I want to, and it often causes consequences that spill over into other areas of my life.

I identified three role models — two friends who seemed to be naturally calm and thoughtful, and a third who clearly works at keeping himself composed. And of course, as my mentor suggested, I included myself as a role model — focusing on those rare occasions I held myself together in the face of adversity. Though I only managed to observe, without speaking to, one of the two "naturals" during this short time, I did have the chance to speak with the third, in full confidence, about his strategies.

I feel good about the process. Clearly, it needs *way* more than one day's time, and I look forward to pursuing and learning from others throughout my life. But for the purposes of getting me to think of specific, doable actions, it certainly did the job.

"LET ME TELL you the story about the amulet," my mentor began today's meeting. He always had seemed like a rational man, so his mention of amulets completely threw me off.

Sitting back in his chair in a reminiscent posture, looking past me, my mentor continued.

"There was a young man who had a terrible time handling criticism. Now, to be sure," he added, quickly glancing back at me, "no one likes to be criticized. But this fellow was particularly vulnerable to it, because of his personal history of rejection and all... and he needed a strategy badly."

He returned to his distant gaze, "Life was unbearable — especially at home. He would simply fall apart every time his wife sent the slightest signal of discontent, let alone when she would get outright nasty!"

"Sounds familiar," I thought aloud.

"What do you mean?"

"I mean the young man's reaction," I quickly explained.

"His weakness is almost identical to the one I found in myself!"

"Well, then this example should resonate very well with you." My mentor commented, as he continued with the story.

"Of course, it took the young man a while to own up to his vulnerability. At first, when I asked about his overly forceful reactions, he would say, 'Well, wouldn't *you* be upset if your wife criticized you?' To which I would answer, 'Sure, but not nearly as much as you!'

"Anyway, I pulled out an index card. Nothing fancy, just a plain index card. I asked him to write, at the top, a brief description of the type of situation that gets him angry, starting his sentence with the words "I get angry when..." Then I had him describe the dysfunctional ways he usually would respond. I told him not to be offended by the word dysfunctional. I meant it with a lower case "d" as a description of an unhelpful reaction, rather than one that necessarily requires serious intervention.

"Then I asked him to think of ways he would prefer to react—what he would consider to be a 'functional,' appropriate reaction. Then we wrote those target behaviors on the card."

MY MENTOR SAT up and looked at me straight in the eye. "But it was not enough to write the behaviors. We needed to capture the functional thoughts — how he should *think,* and what would be his motivation.

"I asked him, 'What do you have to tell yourself in order to have the strength to implement those effective behaviors? What should you be thinking? What attitude do you need to adopt? What values do you believe in that would mandate better behavior? What is your personal philosophy?' And I asked him to write those down."

He scribbled a few words on an index card and then he turned it in my direction. "It looked something like this:"

I get angry when... my wife criticizes me and raises her voice.

I think: 1. This is not about me; I will survive this.
2. Strength is in self-control.
3. She needs me to be strong.
4. I can do it.

I react by: 1. Taking deep breaths
2. Focusing on my breath
3. Not saying anything

I read it quietly.

Looking up from the card, my mentor added:

"Keep in mind that there are many varieties of functional and motivational thinking. For example, you can give meaning to the target behavior by doing it in memory of a loved one. Or, you can add symbolism to it. There was a certain woman who had an aversion to flossing. The underlying issues that held her back are unimportant for our purposes, but in order to make a commitment to flossing that would be inspiring enough for her to carry it through, she sought to imbue it with more profound meaning. She looked for a frame, a philosophy—a dental *flossify,* you might call it—so that a mundane act like flossing could carry with it the potential to change her life. It could have been something as simple as seeing plaque as an enemy of her choice, perhaps a negative personal trait, and flossing symbolic of conquering that enemy. In that way, her commitment would have an impact that would far exceed merely having healthy gums. She would be a woman with a mission!"

And with that, my mentor returned my attention to the card.

"Notice how he writes 'I think...' and 'I react by...' in the present tense. This is because the card is intended to replace his mind's old, dysfunctional soundtrack with a new one, and it describes success as though it is already happening."

I nodded.

"I told him to keep the card in his shirt pocket and pull

it out in case of emergency. And with that, he went on his way.

"Within a day, I had already heard about his first success. His wife had begun to criticize him. In a panic, he realized that he had left his card in the bedroom, so he quickly asked her to wait as he ran to get it. He returned in a flash, quietly scanned his instructions, and kept his composure."

"Didn't it frustrate his wife to see him looking at a card and not at her?" I asked.

"On the contrary," the mentor responded. "The wife was so impressed she begged him to tell her what was written on the card. But the husband kept it a secret, only sharing with her his desire and determination to be more supportive of her at times like that."

"Amazing...," I said, "but, why do you call it an amulet?"

"Well, the wife had no other explanation for the effect the card had on her husband than to assume it was some magical charm, some kind of amulet. Since then, there has been steady improvement, and she still has no idea what is written on that card."

I was impressed by the story, largely because of how such a simple intervention can enable such profound growth. My mentor noted my admiration and offered an explanation.

"When you have done the ground work for change — when you have identified your motivation to change and the behaviors needed to make that change happen — success simply becomes a matter of making yourself aware of it all at your moment of challenge! It's all about self-awareness and self-talk. And this simple card serves those purposes. I call it a "Personal Success Card."

At this point, I realized how this card could be, in fact, the culmination of all of my work.

"So, you're saying that I should draw up an index card of my own where I identify the type of event that triggers my negative reactions and then jot down my motivations — a viable thought process for change, and the functional behavior I need to adopt."

"That's right," he responded. "And don't forget to include, among your motivations, your desire to be close to G-d, the frame we have described for all meaningful growth, as well as your regrets for having acted wrongly in the past."

With that, I set off to my home, prepared to make magic happen with an amulet of my own.

STEP 8: Write your personal success card.

- *I [have a problem] when...*
- *To change my behavior, I need to think...*
- *And react by...*

STEP 9

Focus on Core Traits

IN PREPARATION FOR THE next step, my mentor took me back to a prior discussion. "Do you remember when you felt overwhelmed by the weight of the many sins you had underlined, and the thought of having to spend many lifetimes repairing them all?"

"How could I forget?"

I recalled that at the time, he had shared one thought of encouragement, and now he felt it was time to share the other.

"I'm sure you've heard of the concept of collateral damage."

I nodded.

"Well, today I would like to speak to you about collateral benefits. We often find ourselves in relationships that seem to be, pardon the expression, hemorrhaging: there are so many problems that we do not even know where to begin the healing. It can happen in a marriage; it can happen in parenting. Husbands and wives, parents and children can feel, as you do, that it would take many lifetimes to address all of the issues between them.

"But in most cases, our many presenting problems stem from no more than a handful of root causes. And if we were to get in the habit of focusing on our core issues, we could heal many of our problems at once.

"When we become aware of this, our work suddenly becomes very manageable. After all, it's very encouraging to know that one behavioral shift can effect many changes. In that case, it is no longer an overwhelming situation at all."

He went on to introduce today's work.

"You are committing to make one significant shift in your life. But your growth should not be limited to that one behavior. At the end of the year, when you look back at all the times you controlled your temper, you will have much more than a year with less conflict.

"In other words, by addressing one area directly, you will be deriving many collateral benefits along the way. Today's assignment is to identify all the gains you will acquire by meeting your goal."

That was food for thought. If I keep my commitment to change, what would be all of the side benefits? But I wasn't quite sure what he meant, so I asked for an example.

"Okay, let's say you decide to pray from a *siddur*, instead of from memory. The benefits could range from the direct benefit of improving *kavanah* (by looking at the words) to an indirect benefit of combating laziness (by making an effort to go get the *siddur*). If you find every way your resolution would lift you, you might improve in many other areas that you had not even considered when designing your resolution."

"So," I began to summarize, "what you are saying is that one resolution could actually address many of my deficiencies—like a domino effect—and could, in the long run, reduce the time I need to perfect myself by several lifetimes!"

"That's right," he confirmed. "And here is the most important concept to consider: When you set a goal for yourself, your greatest achievement is not so much in what you will *have,* but what you will *become*—responsible, compassionate, caring, passionate about life! Ultimately, growth is all about changing our character, which is part of the essence of who we are. And once you make a change in your character, you will be able to do all kinds of things you could not do before.

So it's important to write the traits you will be acquiring through your behavior change on the card, too. After all, that is the big prize at the end of the line."

My mentor showed me how this would look for the man with the "amulet" we had talked about in our last meeting.

I get angry when... my wife criticizes me and raises her voice.

I think: 1. This is not about me; I will survive this.
2. Strength is in self-control.
3. She needs me to be strong.
4. I can do it.

I react by: 1. Taking deep breaths
2. Focusing on my breath
3. Not saying anything

And I am: Disciplined, Confident, Patient, Calm

"This," my mentor continued, "is really the basis of your motivation to change. It follows the model of advertisers, those masters of motivation..."

I wondered where he was going with this.

"YOU KNOW THAT advertisers do not actually sell things. After all, how attractive is a pack of lethal cigarettes to someone who has any value for life? What they are really selling is what you will *become* if you buy their product, and they can make that very attractive. You have a man riding on a horse who exudes manliness, and the consumer believes that buying that brand of cigarettes will turn him into the masculine man he desperately yearns to be."

"So the draw is not *smoking* the cigarettes, but *becoming* a man," I repeated.

"That's right. And in a similar vein, we must keep our eye on the ultimate goal when making our resolutions... what we will *become* through our behavior changes."

I sat back to take it all in, but he was on a roll.

"AT THE SAME time, you should also keep your eye on an image of yourself acting in the way that your success card describes. For example, if your goal is to be calm, think of a time that you were calm. The key is to envision yourself being the way you want to be, regardless of what the specific circumstances happen to be."

"Do you mean like the time I lost my wallet?" I asked.

"How did you react?"

"Calmly," I replied. "Surprisingly, I stayed very composed. It was strange. My wallet contained a lot of cash and other valuables, but somehow a state of calm prevailed over me."

"That's perfect. And for the young man in our story, it is when he reads on his porch on a warm summer day."

"But how is that helpful if his calm was not challenged at all?" I argued.

"It doesn't matter," my mentor answered. "You can step into any calm image you have of yourself, regardless of the circumstances, as I said before. Now, once you have the moment, create an image of yourself, whether reacting calmly to the news of the lost wallet or just placidly reading on the porch, and capture it. Then, give it a title and record it on your card. For that young man, it looked something like this."

My mentor picked up his pen and completed the final line on the index card.

I get angry when... my wife criticizes me and raises her voice.
I think: 1. This is not about me; I will survive this.
2. Strength is in self-control.
3. She needs me to be strong.
4. I can do it.
I react by: 1. Taking deep breaths
2. Focusing on my breath
3. Not saying anything
And I am: Disciplined, Confident, Patient, Calm
Like when... I am reading a book on the porch.

"With this last piece, your amulet will not only have the verbal instructions describing what you need to do when the trigger happens, but you will also have a point of reference with an image that you can step into. And in some ways, that image can be worth more than a thousand other words on the card."

As I processed all of what my mentor was saying, I made a remarkable discovery. "Do you mean to say that the specific problem that I chose to work on — my angry reactions to my wife's raised voice — is merely a symptom of a more profound problem?"

He nodded.

"So if I want to make a permanent change, I need to focus on the root of the problem. Once I get to the core and rectify it, my actions will be more appropriate in many areas."

"You got it," he confirmed. The ultimate goal of *teshuvah* is to work on our character. And that leads us to today's final point."

"AS YOU ACHIEVE success in the specific challenge area you have chosen to work on, you can begin to **'future pace.'** This means that as you gain control of your reactions in your home — the "trigger" on your card — you can begin to identify other situations that bring out the worst in you — and you'll recognize that these can be licked by the same thoughts and attitudes, behaviors and character traits that rendered successes. It's another dimension of the domino effect."

Looking at the card, I thought out loud. "So, for this man to future pace, he would look for other situations in his life where he lacks self-control and confidence and then write a card for them..."

"Exactly," he replied, "together with the thoughts and attitudes that helped create that way of being."

"And where do I record the new trigger?"

"On a new card..."

"And when would you say is the time to add a new card?"

"That all depends on your pace of growth. But that too may be a goal you want to set: let's say, one card per month. This will add a little incentive to work hard at mastering a trigger within a specific time frame..."

I tried to imagine what it would be like to be carrying a deck of success cards to *shul* next Rosh Hashanah. How satisfying it would feel, and how much more confident I would be in making my case to G-d, asking Him to invest in me for another year...

STEP 9: Focus on core traits: Identify your target character trait and strengthen it with an image of success.

Add to your card:

- *And I am ___ (targeted character trait)*
- *Like when ___ (image of success)*

STEP 10

Get Rid of Obstacles

THIS WAS IT, MY last meeting with my mentor! After nine days of tiring work, I stood ready to receive my final charge. I started to thank him for being so gracious with his time and generous with his insight, but he was not open to my appreciation until the job was done. He went straight to today's topic.

"Your resolution is well-formed and you have the motivation to make it happen. All you have left to do is predict and address the obstacles that may potentially block you from keeping your commitment."

He told me to think about what has caused, and could continue to cause, me to lose control at home. For starters, I came up with the following possibilities: Bringing my problems home with me from work; not getting enough sleep; and taking on too many tasks at once.

"Once you have identified all of the challenges, come up

with solutions for each one and make them a part of your commitment."

For starters, I knew I needed some way to release the tensions of my workday before coming home; and get to sleep earlier; and maybe even invest in a handyman to free me up from the stresses of home ownership and improvement.

I mentioned these possibilities to my mentor and he felt confident that I got his point.

HE THEN TOOK the time to explain an important concept relating to today's topic. He said that whenever a part of us generates undesirable behavior (for example, our greedy self, our procrastinating self, our loud self) there is usually a positive intention to that part. But without our awareness of that positive underlying intention, the resulting behavior becomes our biggest obstacle to growth.

He shared a story to illustrate his point.

There was a certain man who had come to him complaining how his "stupid" self keeps getting him into trouble with his wife. The man described how he gets too persistent trying to get his wife to spend time together with him, and that it makes his wife crazy.

"I'm so *stupid*," the man said, "and I wish I could just get rid of that stupid side of me. She needs her space and I just cannot give it to her!"

My mentor, following the principle of positive intention, guided the man to find the motivation for his "stupid" self. In the end, the fellow made the following discovery: As a young couple, he and his wife had spent considerable time together. But as time went on, they each got steadily busier, to the point that they were slowly drifting apart. This triggered a reaction within him (for abandonment happened to be a familiar experience from his past, but that is a different story.) Now, instead of seeing his coercive reaction as being wholly bad, he came to realize that its underlying drive was noble: he wanted to preserve his connection with his wife. He had been calling the part of himself that had responded to their separation "stupid," but was now able to reframe it as the "guardian of the relationship."

What made it "stupid" was not its intention, but its intensity. "Stupid" was really a very important voice, only it needed to be integrated with his "smart" self so that it could react more thoughtfully. The goal was not to eliminate the good intention, but to modify it to a practical, effective level.

"It's all about integration, not elimination," is how my mentor summed it all up. "And as long as one operates with an attitude of elimination ('I must uproot this behavior — motivation and all!'), the direction toward healing will be all wrong. After all, as long as 'stupid' remains 'stupid,' the man focuses his work on resigning to the growing gap in the relationship, rather than trying to reconnect with wisdom."

I contemplated the concept and thought of how it applied to me. According to this idea, the part of me that causes me to explode at home has an inner voice with something valuable to say, and that it is important for me to listen to that message. I should not just assume it is bad and needs to be eliminated. This, my mentor emphasized, is the basis for "congruent growth" — growth that is experienced by one's entire being.

"There is only one part of the body that has no positive purpose in one's growth and that is removed at the *bris.* Every other part," he said, "physical or emotional, has its place and its positive purpose."

This idea took me to a thought I'd had on the fourth day of this journey. Back then, when I was contemplating not going back to my mentor, I fortified myself with love of G-d, and managed to make my way out of the car, leaving what I called, my *procrastinating* self with all of its uncertainties behind. And, as I walked towards my mentor's front door, I felt as though I had walked away from a part of myself that I was wholly determined to bring me to *defeat.*

Those were fighting words! But, from what my mentor just said, I am *not* supposed to defeat the cynical self. I am supposed to listen to it, find its positive intention, and then invite it into my growth plan. At that point, I would have my whole being working towards the same goal — a situation that has the best odds for success.

But what could that be?

This kind of reflection needs time, and I was not about to dig so deeply on the spot. But some thoughts did flash through my mind: maybe the "positive intention" behind my resistance to continuing with my mentor stemmed from excessive humility. But it was not a healthy form of humility, for it emerged as a lack of confidence.

Maybe I do not value myself enough to think that I was worthy of his time. And maybe my tendency to depend on someone else without giving myself a chance to use my own wisdom stems from that same lack of confidence. Maybe my *procrastinating self* is a "positive intention," in itself, because it was not really trying to stop me from doing *teshuvah*, but from becoming too dependent on the wisdom of others. Maybe it was telling me to think for myself, trust myself, invest in myself. These contemplations may not do much for others, but they were sure making sense to me.

JUST THEN, I remembered an exchange I had with my mentor back on our third meeting, but had not recorded in this journal. I did not consider its message significant until now.

In our first meeting, he indicated that he would not need more than a few minutes a session to teach me his plan for growth, but that if I had any other matters to discuss with him, he would find time for them as well.

Well, on day three, I decided to share with him a life dilemma that had come up. It was a complex question that required me to make an important decision — and it would carry serious consequences. His first response took me by surprise: he asked what *I* had thought about it. I was taken aback.

After all, wasn't it obvious that I felt incapable of rendering a decision for myself, which is why I was bringing it to him? But he persisted: "Go home and use your wisdom to think it over; then, let me know what you come up with and we can discuss it further."

"Use your wisdom"... have confidence. ...Yes, perhaps my *procrastinating self* did have something important to say to me. And he had perceived this early on.

All of this raced through my mind in moments. I did not feel the need to check it out with my mentor. Its truth was so clear to me that it needed no outside validation. In fact, that very confidence is a priceless byproduct of my association with him.

We both stood up to walk towards the front door.

"WELL, YOU MADE it," said my mentor, as he gave me a congratulatory pat on my shoulder. "You have reached the end of a simple, yet challenging journey. How do you feel?"

I thought for a brief moment before confirming that I felt spent, but ready.

"It was tough, but I'm still standing!" was how I put it.

"That makes sense. You know, experts in goal-setting say that in order to make an effective plan for change one must invest no less than ten hours in the process.

"As we have seen, they were right with the number, but off with the measure of time. The Torah says it takes ten *days* to make a plan. During *Aseres Y'mei Teshuvah,* G-d gives us the motivation, the atmosphere, and the framework we need to make that happen. So it makes sense that we think of change during these times.

"But it's important to remember that this growth plan is relevant all year long. The season of *teshuvah*, prompted by the birthday of mankind, is the universal impetus for improvement. But anyone can decide to change, to reach for this roadmap any time he feels inspired—whether that inspiration comes from a personal birthday, a milestone event, a complaint by a spouse, or anything else that gets one going."

"So," I observed, "it really wasn't *necessary* for me to have imposed upon you on the day before Rosh Hashanah to discuss your plan, as had been my concern when we first met... nor did I *have* to wait a full eleven months since that fateful *Ne'ilah* before working towards change."

"As you now know," he affirmed, "change is a year-round experience."

I MADE A mental note then that if I were to publish my notes in the form of a personal journal, I could not refer to it as protocol for *Aseres Y'mei Teshuvah.* No, that would box it into just those ten days and make it seem to the reader that it's irrelevant for the rest of the year.

I also sensed that using the term *teshuvah,* even without reference to the Days of Awe, would create the same stifling effect.

Instead, I'll have to find a way to intimate that the value of this ten-step plan truly transcends any one time and space. It's a roadmap for anyone who recognizes his need to grow, anyone who earnestly wants to be a better person, but wonders, "How can I change, for Heaven's sake?"

But I put that thought aside for the moment and struggled to express my gratitude to my mentor.

"I have no words to thank you for all you have done for me. Simply put, you have changed my life," I said, as I stretched my hand out towards my mentor.

But he bypassed the handshake. The profound relationship we had developed made that too trivial. Instead, he chose an embrace.

"You have grown," he began, "and you will continue to grow. You have a plan in your hands that is sure to succeed. Just stay with it and, with G-d's help, you will be standing at this time, next year, with great confidence, knowing that you have made a real change in your life. So I understand your appreciation and I accept your kind words."

He had allowed me the pleasure of thanking him and I was grateful to him for that. It was important to me that he should realize how thankful I was to him. And as I took a step back, ready to return to my car, he continued, "and I must thank you, too. You have given me an opportunity to share a process that is very precious to me and that I get great pleasure teaching to others. I told you that when we first met.

"I also want to thank you for inspiring me with your honesty and enthusiasm, your persistence and determination. If I, as a mere mentor, had so much *nachas* watching you struggle and grow, I cannot begin to imagine how much more *nachas* G-d had watching you."

I was touched by his words. I had not perceived our interaction as being of mutual benefit. Typical of me, I guess. I always felt a need to apologize for imposing on him; it goes back to that lack of confidence, I suppose. I was ready to deflect his words, my usual way of dealing with compliments. Instead, I learned my final lesson from him — and accepted the compliment.

"I understand your appreciation and I graciously accept your kind words."

And on that note, we wished each other the best, and parted ways.

STEP 10: Recognize "positive intentions" and get rid of obstacles.

STRATEGIES: Ask yourself:

- *What holds me back from being the way I want to be?*
- *What can I do to neutralize that obstacle?*
- *[If the obstacle is a force within me] what positive intention might underlie the resistance it presents?*
- *How can I satisfy that positive intention so that it no longer sabotages my goal?*

A New Year's Revolution

...IT HAD BEEN A long, hard, and backbreaking day, with four prayers down and only one to go. The rabbi, draped in his *talis*, solemnly stepped towards the pulpit to deliver the year's most meaningful message. The drama of the moment was written all over his face, and on those of his anxious congregants who were sitting up and ready to hear their charge. And as the rabbi uttered his first words, it all started to sink in.

"The gates are closing. This is the time to make your commitments!" beckoned the rabbi. "Make this final confession during these closing moments of Yom Kippur your most sincere..."

One man heard the words "commitments" and "most sincere" and he nodded in agreement, getting ready to "roll up his sleeves" to face the task at hand. He realized that "commitments" and "most sincere confessions" are the products of focused energy and lots of hard work. This year, his drive and inspiration were stronger than ever before.

He stood prepared, ready for the enormity of the *Ne'ilah* experience. In short, he felt that he belonged to that holy and awesome moment.

Just then he reminded himself of his painful experience just one year earlier, when the imagery of the weakening sun and the closing gates caused him to kick himself for letting all those days go by without working towards this fateful moment. He had asked himself why he had not prepared properly since the beginning of Elul, as he should have. He had yearned for the opportunity to do them all over again as he stood so hopelessly embarrassed before his Creator.

With great relief, he brought himself back to the present moment. This year, with a series of worksheets detailing the work he had done towards this year's *teshuvah* and a card with a solid commitment which he had thought through so thoroughly, he could declare honestly that things would be different this year. He could complete this day with more confidence.

And so it was that the rabbi had succeeded in just the way that he had intended. He got that man ready to cry, with real tears. But, unlike last year, these tears were not tears of despair; they were the sweat of his soul, for he had worked so hard to prepare himself for this awesome moment. And, unlike last year, he would not have to think of asking G-d to grant him atonement on credit. Instead, he would recite his personal prayer for the last time, and offer his plan for spiritual growth in an effort to convince G-d that he is worth the investment of another year of health, wealth and all the other wonderful blessings. And, as the rabbi stepped down from the pulpit, the man with the tears stood ready to "make the final confession of those precious last moments of these days his most meaningful..."

WHILE THE MAN had achieved a great deal and had gained so much confidence in his approach to change, he knew to remain humble. It would have been so easy for him to look around and pity those who struggled, and to feel superior to them as he moved ahead with a purpose and plan. But he was well aware that a plan that frames progress within the context of a relationship with G-d has no tolerance for such an attitude. It demands humility, and he worked hard at staying that course.

He also knew that the process of growth would never be easy. Sure, success is motivating; but the work remains work. In fact, the man was still overwhelmed at the prospect of properly dealing with the personal challenges of the ensuing year. But he prayed to G-d for help to build on his success and to give him the strength to do what he now knew he must do.

And as he offered up this prayer, he did so with confidence that it would be received in good grace... after all, he was simply seeking Divine assistance to change, for Heaven's sake.

One year later...

Postcript: "We Can Change... for Heaven's Sake!"

THE SHOFAR HAS JUST been blown for the first time this season. It's the reminder to start thinking about *teshuvah* again. And I am ready. After all, I have a plan. But more importantly, I have tasted success. Yes, you can add "prophet" to my mentor's resume. I *am* standing here, as he predicted, encouraged and confident, knowing that I have made real changes in my life in the past year... supported by the deck of success cards in my hand.

It wasn't easy. There were times during the year that I felt like slacking off and giving up. But, at the same time, I also knew that those were the times that I needed to generate an extra dose of motivation, and hang in there with the awareness that, as long as I stay in the game, I will be in position to reignite the passion that would propel me to the finish line. After all, ups and downs are a part of the pulsation of life, and the key is never to give up.

At certain points of the year, I even went so far as to temporarily adjust my commitment—either in its frequency or intensity. But I never gave it up completely, because I knew intuitively that if I would give up, I would lose it all. And I was determined not to let that happen.

But I'm not writing this entry to gloat, Heaven forbid. I am writing it to share an answer to a question that is asked by so many at this time of the year: How can we be truly remorseful in our confessions, promising to change when we know—full well—that we will cry over the same sins every year?

I struggled with this question for a while, as many do. Along the way, I heard the following story:

The story was of a delinquent teen riding in a subway car who was scratching his initials into its windows with the teeth of a key. No one was paying much attention to him except for a man who was sitting in the seat directly across the aisle. As the man watched the vandalizing teen doing his thing, he got increasingly filled with anger. "What a chutzpah!" he thought, but kept it to himself. It was only when the teen looked up from his work and turned towards the man, that the man was able to give him a strong look of disapproval.

And then, something happened. At that moment, the teen—apparently struck with inexplicable remorse—licked his finger and tried his best to undo the damage that he had done. Of course, it was to no avail. The scratch marks remained unchanged. But, as it turned out, his efforts did change something—it changed the man's attitude. Suddenly, instead of feeling enraged at the wayward teen, he felt pity for him. He even found himself wishing that he had some way to help the poor kid...

And with this story comes an answer to our question. Although we may sometimes feel that our *teshuvah* is futile, that we are unable to make any changes to our behavior, we may very well, in our futility, be "changing" the way G-d looks at us. As we desperately rub the scratch marks, we may be causing G-d to be less angry and more merciful, and even want to reach out to help us.

What an accomplishment that would be: it would surely constitute *teshuvah*, if not *kaparah*, with all of its benefits!

For some time now, I had been content with this insight and reassured by it each year I felt I was starting Elul from "scratch."

But this year I discovered an even better way to deal with the problem. I recognized that the premise of the question is false. We *can* change. There is no reason why we should be standing from year to year in the same stationary position. We just have to have a plan and do the work, day by day, without relying on a last minute rally in the closing moments of *Ne'ilah* to hold us for the year.

That is how change happens. And it is within the reach of anyone who really wants it...for Heaven's sake.

The Roadmap
A SUMMARY

STEP 1
Reflect on Your Relationship with G-d

STEP 2
Formulate the Frame

STEP 3
Take Stock

STEP 4
Use Regret Constructively

STEP 5
Find Your Growth Edge

STEP 6
Find Effective Thoughts and Attitudes

STEP 7
Identify Target Behaviors

STEP 8
Write Your Personal Success Card

STEP 9
Focus on Core Traits

STEP 10
Recognize "Positive Intentions" and Get Rid of Obstacles

My Roadmap: Charting My Own Course

STEP 1: Reflect on your relationship with G-d.

My relationship with G-d is important to me because...
Or, I feel impelled to be closer to G-d because...

STEP 2: Formulate the frame.

(a) The way I would characterize my dream relationship with G-d is...

(b) The way that achieving this relationship would improve my life is...

Or, the way I would think, act, and feel differently when I have that relationship is...

____

____

____

STEP 3: Take stock.

(Survey this Yom Kippur Viduy list and chunk down as many stock items as you can by specifying how you may have violated them.)

For the sin we committed before you...

1. **Accidentally and willingly**
   Specifically, by...

   ____

2. **With hard-heartedness**
   Specifically, by...

   ____

3. **By not using our intellectual capabilities**
   Specifically, by...

   ____

4. **With verbal expression**
   Specifically, by...

   ____

5. **Overtly and covertly**
   Specifically, by...

   ____

6. **Through illicit relationships**
   Specifically, by...

   ___

7. **Through speech**
   Specifically, by...

   ___

8. **Knowledgeably and deceitfully**
   Specifically, by...

   ___

9. **With thought**
   Specifically, by...

   ___

10. **Through injustice to a fellow Jew**
    Specifically, by...

    ___

11. **Through mere oral confession**
    Specifically, by...

    ___

12. **By joining a gathering of levity between genders**
    Specifically, by...

    ___

13. **Intentionally and unintentionally**
    Specifically, by...

    ___

14. **In showing insufficient respect to parents and teachers**
    Specifically, by...

    ___

15. Through use of compulsion
Specifically, by...

____

16. By desecrating G-d's Name
Specifically, by...

____

17. Through foolishness of the mouth
Specifically, by...

____

18. With impurity of the lips
Specifically, by...

____

19. With the evil inclination
Specifically, by...

____

20. Knowingly and unknowingly
Specifically, by...

____

21. By compelling others through bribery
Specifically, by...

____

22. By yielding to the pressure imposed by a bribe
Specifically, by...

____

23. Through false denial and false promise
Specifically, by...

____

24. **Through slander**
    Specifically, by...

    ____

25. **In business**
    Specifically, by...

    ____

26. **Through food and drink**
    Specifically, by...

    ____

27. **Through all types of usury**
    Specifically, by...

    ____

28. **Through acting haughtily**
    Specifically, by...

    ____

29. **Through misuse of the eyes**
    Specifically, by...

    ____

30. **Through lip service**
    Specifically, by...

    ____

31. **Through pride**
    Specifically, by...

    ____

32. **By having a brazen face**
    Specifically, by...

    ____

33. **Through insubordination**
Specifically, by...

34. **In court matters**
Specifically, by...

35. **By stalking a fellow Jew**
Specifically, by...

36. **Through small-mindedness**
Specifically, by...

37. **Through light-mindedness**
Specifically, by...

38. **Through stubbornness**
Specifically, by...

39. **By running to do evil**
Specifically, by...

40. **By talebearing**
Specifically, by...

41. **By making a wasted oath**
Specifically, by...

42. By unjustified hatred
Specifically, by...

____

43. By monetary abuse
Specifically, by...

____

44. In a state of confusion
Specifically, by...

____

(See Chayei Adam and Viduy of the Chidah, as cited on p. 125, for ways by which they have chunked down the "Ashamnu" viduy. You can use either of their lists to take stock as well.)

STEP 4: Use regret constructively.

(a) The reason it is bad to violate G-d's will, in general, is...

____

____

(b) The reason I feel bad having ______________ ***is...***
[A STOCK ITEM FROM STEP 3]

____

____

(c) The damage that I did to others by behaving that way is...

____

____

(d) The way that behaving that way has pulled me down is...

____

____

(e) The way that being that way has kept me from achieving ______________________ is...

[MY GLOBAL DESIRE FROM STEP 2A–B]

____

____

STEP 5: **Find your growth edge.**

(a) One shortcoming of mine that I have heard people complain about is...

____

____

____

(b) I would be a changed person if I were the opposite, namely, if I had the trait of ______________________

[TARGET TRAIT]

(c) Some of the stock items from step 3 that were a result of my having this shortcoming include...

- ______________________________________
- ______________________________________
- ______________________________________
- ______________________________________

STEP 6: Find effective thoughts and attitudes.

(a) What goes through your (or your role model's) mind when being ____________________________ is...

[TARGET TRAIT FROM 5B]

____

____

____

(b) What is important to you (or your role model) about being that way is...

____

____

____

(c) The philosophy behind the desire to be that way is...

____

____

____

STEP 7: Identify target behaviors.

What specifically you (or the role model) do when being ____________________________ is...

[TARGET TRAIT FROM 5B]

(This can include the way [the role model] moves, stands, communicates — both in word and tone — or acts when he is being that way.)

____

____

____

STEPS 8: **Write your personal success card.**

(Write the answers to a–c on the success card below)

(a) The target situation that challenges you, based on a stock item from 5c)...

(b) To be effective, I think and tell myself... (Include motivational thoughts, directive thoughts, insight and philosophies from step 6a–c)

(c) I react by... (based on step 7)

When... (8a)

I think and tell myself... (8b)

I react by... (8c)

And I am ... (9a)

Like when ... (9b)

STEPS 9: **Focus on core traits.**

(Write the answers to [a] and [b] on the success card above)

(a) And I am... (target trait from step 5b)

(b) Like when... (image of success)

This success card will bring me to ________________________
[MY GLOBAL DESIRE FROM STEP 2A–B]
in that...

____

____

____

____

My collateral benefits from carrying out the success card include...

____

____

____

____

STEP 10: Recognize "positive intentions" and get rid of obstacles.

What holds me back from following my success card is...

____

____

____

What I can do to neutralize that obstacle is...

____

____

____

(If the obstacle is a force within me,) the positive intention that might underlie the resistance it presents is...

Another way that I can satisfy that positive intention so that it no longer sabotages my goal is...

(Note that this awareness can be added to your success card under "I think and tell myself")

Future pacing – 2 ways

I can step up my current commitment (i.e. level of frequency, challenge) by...

Another area of my life where I can write a new success card, applying my new effective thoughts, behaviors, and character traits is...

Second success card

When...

I think and tell myself...

I react by...

And I am ...

Like when ...

Sources

1. **The roadmap** — Rambam (*Mishneh Torah,* Laws of *Teshuvah,* 1:1)
2. **Distinction between *teshuvah* and New Year's resolutions; distinction between *teshuvah* and *kaparah*** — Rabbi Yaakov Weinberg
3. **Global desire** — Rabbi Chaim Friedlander (*Sifsei Chaim,* Mo'ados, Volume I, p. 90)
4. **Chunking down transgressions** — See *Chayei Adam,* by Rabbi Avraham Danzig (Laws of Yom Kippur, 143:1) and *Viduy* of the *Chidah,* brought in *Siddur Otzar HaTefilos,* towards the end of volume II.
5. **Knowing yourself, finding your growth edge** — Rabbi Shlomo Wolbe (*Alei Shur,* Volume I, p. 65)
6. **Targeting a character trait** — Rambam (*Mishneh Torah,* Laws of *Teshuvah,* 7:3)
7. **Consult with a comrade** — Rabbeinu Yonah (*Commentary on Pirkei Avos,* 1:6, on acquiring a friend)

8. **Integration versus elimination** — Rabbi Eliyahu of Vilna (*Commentary on Mishlei,* 22:6)

9. **Positive intention** — Rabbi Yehudah HaLevi, (*Kuzari,* First *Ma'amar*)

10. **Staying resilient during down times** — Rabbeinu Tam (*Sefer HaYashar,* quoted in *Alei Shur,* Volume I, pp. 34–35)

Glossary

(All foreign words are Hebrew, unless indicated otherwise)

AKEIDAH: the "binding of Isaac" on a sacrificial alter by Abraham (Genesis 22:1–19)

"AL CHET" VIDUY: oral confession said on Yom Kippur

ASERES Y'MEI TESHUVAH: the Ten Days of Repentance, from Rosh Hashanah to Yom Kippur

"ASHAMNU" VIDUY: oral confession said on Yom Kippur that proceeds in alphabetical order

BA'AL TESHUVAH: one who has repented

BREISHIS: Biblical book of Genesis

CHASID: a devotee of a Chasidic Rabbi

ELUL: twelfth and final month of the Jewish calendar; a time to prepare for repentance before the upcoming High Holy Days

FAST OF GEDALIAH: fast day that immediately follows Rosh Hashanah

HAVDALAH: the ceremony performed at the end of the Sabbath or a holiday to distinguish it from the rest of the days of the week

KAPARAH: cleansing (related to sin)

KAVANAH: intention; concentrated focus

LASHON HARA: gossip

L'DAVID HASHEM ORI: first three words of Psalm 27, customarily recited from the first of Elul through the holiday of Sukkos

MACHZOR: prayer book used on Jewish holidays

MINYAN: prayer quorum of ten male adults

MISHNAH: part of the Talmud

MITZVOS: commandments

NACHAS: joy

NE'ILAH: fifth and final prayer service of Yom Kippur

POTIPHAR: Joseph's master when he was sold as a slave in Egypt (Genesis 39:1)

RAMBAM: Hebrew acronym for Rabbi Moshe ben Maimon, a.k.a. Maimonides

ROSH HAYESHIVAH: dean of a yeshivah (school of Judaic studies)

SCHLEP: (Yiddish) drag

SELICHOS: special prayers of supplication said before and during the High Holiday season

SHUCKLE: (Yiddish) to sway, usually during prayers

SHUL: (Yiddish) synagogue

TALIS: prayer shawl

TESHUVAH: repentance

YAMIM NORA'IM: Days of Awe, specifically Rosh Hashanah and Yom Kippur